LIMHI
SON OF NOAH

LIMHI
SON OF NOAH

Pamela Lents Robison

Herald Publishing House
Independence, Missouri

Copyright © 1989
Herald Publishing House
Independence, Missouri
Printed in the United States of America

All rights in this book are reserved. No part of the text may be reproduced in any form without written permission of the publisher, except brief quotations used in connection with reviews in magazines or newspapers.

Robison, Pamela Kaye.
   Limhi, son of Noah / by Pamela Lents Robison.
      p.   cm.
   Summary: A retelling of the Book of Mormon story of how Limhi, one of the sons of King Noah, determines to do what he thinks is right against all odds.
   ISBN 0-8309-0558-8
   1. Limhi (Book of Mormon character)—Juvenile literature. 2. Book of Mormon stories. [1. Limhi (Book of Mormon character) 2. Book of Mormon stories.] I. Title.
BX8627.A2R63   1989
289.3'22—dc20   89-27289
                                                          CIP
                                                           AC

ISBN 0-8309-0558-8

Chapter 1

The king was angry. Noah paced the floor, kicking at anything and anyone in his way. Small groups of people cowered in corners, whispering together—but the whispers stopped whenever Noah came close.

Finally he stumped back to his throne and threw himself down. He glared around the room, bellowing, "Get out of here, all of you! Get out! Get out!"

There was a mad dash to the door as people scurried out of the throne room. Each person hurried to get as far away from the king as possible.

Noah slumped in his throne. "Where is he?" he muttered. "Where is Barak? He *must* return with Alma!" He paused, thinking. "Nothing's been the same since that...that madman was here. He corrupted so many of my people."

Nothing moved. Shadows began to lengthen, making the room darker. The king remained slumped, lost in thought.

Finally he jerked upright. "Omer...Omer... where are you?" There was no response. Noah rose and his voice grew louder. "Omer!"

The door opened tentatively, and a little man slith-

5

ered in. He quickly came toward Noah, bowing as low as possible.

"Oh, most gracious king. What is your command?"

"Shut up, you fool!" Noah began pacing again. "Where is Barak? Is there no sign of him yet?"

"No, most gracious king." The little man made himself as small as possible.

Noah's face flushed bright red and he kicked at Omer. "Go and look again, you idiot! He *must* be coming back!"

Omer eagerly scurried out of the room. Once in the hall he paused, looking back, and then limped slowly down the hall.

As he reached the front of the palace, Omer looked to the distance. There was nothing in the air—no dust or other signs of any larger group approaching. He turned to the guard.

"Has there been any word from Barak or Gideon?"

The guard shook his head. "No, lord, nothing."

Omer persisted. "Are you certain? No messenger?"

"No, lord. There has been nothing."

"It has been three days since they left. The king is very concerned—you must let me know the moment you hear anything! Understand?"

The guard looked at Omer. "Yes, lord."

Omer repeated, more emphatically. "The *moment* you hear anything!"

He turned on his heel and returned to the king.

"Most gracious king...."

Noah growled. "Well? What news?"

Omer cringed. "Most gracious king, there is no sign of them, nor any word."

The king clenched his fists and turned his back, muttering to himself. "He must not fail! Barak must not fail me! Alma must be leading a charmed life. I brought him to my court—do you hear me?" the king shouted. "I did! I raised him from the gutter, I gave him prominence and glory—and what did he do in return? He listened to that...that madman! What was his name?"

"Abinadi, sire."

"Abinadi...ever since that man appeared, my life has been turned upside down." His voice fell to a whisper. "Alma deserted me." Suddenly the king raised his voice. "No one deserts me and lives. Even my best...and now, he gathers together many of my people in rebellion. And Barak...Barak is failing...but Barak has never failed me...he will bring him back..."

His voice grew hard. "If he does not, he knows what the punishment for failure is." He paused for a moment and then laughed. "Abinadi promised that I would be burned as he was—demented fool! But he may be right in one way. If Barak has failed me, he will die the same kind of death..."

The king looked through the chamberlain, as though he did not even see him.

"Barak is failing....I can have no pity on those who fail. Those who serve me must understand that. Barak understood..."

Omer waited to see if the king had any further orders for him. But the king had forgotten that he was there, lost in his own thoughts. Omer bowed, turned silently, and tiptoed out of the throne room.

"Omer, what is happening with my father?"

Omer bowed low again to the young man waiting in the hall, but without the fear he had shown in Noah's presence. "Lord Limhi, I'm afraid that the king is worried about Barak's lengthy absence from the court."

7

Limhi laughed. "I would hardly call three days lengthy! Come, Omer, there is more to it than that. Tell me what has happened since I've been gone. I leave to go hunting for several days, and when I return, I find the whole court in an uproar, with no one wishing to attend my father—and all you can tell me is that he is concerned that Barak has been gone for three days?"

Omer looked around the hall. The king had his spies everywhere, and there were few men Omer trusted completely. Limhi was one of them.

"My lord, it would be better if we walked in the garden."

Limhi understood his meaning and responded. "Very well, then."

The two men continued their casual conversation as they made their way to the garden. They made an interesting pair since Omer was short and somewhat hunched over, and Limhi was tall and handsome. The difference in their ages and attitudes was striking as well—Omer, the older, deferring to the younger man.

When Omer and Limhi reached the flower garden, Omer looked around carefully. Limhi noticed this and frowned.

"Omer, what is the problem? Will you please tell me what has happened to make my father so upset—and the court in an uproar?"

"Lord Limhi, do you remember when the king had Abinadi captured and brought to court?"

Limhi nodded impatiently. "Of course, Omer. Who doesn't?"

Omer continued. "You were also aware, were you not, that one of your father's priests, Alma, was banished from the court?"

"Of course. But what does that have to do with...." He stopped suddenly. "Omer, exactly what is the connection between those two activities and what is going on now?"

Omer carefully studied one of the open flowers. "Lord Limhi, Alma was banished because he begged for Abinadi's life to be spared."

"He what?" Limhi was astonished. "Didn't he know what my father would do?"

Omer nodded. "Yes, lord. But he said that he could not deny that Abinadi spoke the truth." Omer stopped, aware that this statement alone could cause his death if Limhi chose to repeat it. The king was vengeful and scared.

Limhi paused a moment. He, too, studied the flowers around him. "Well, Omer, continue. Alma was correct.... He was a fool for giving up what he had here—but he was correct."

Omer discovered that he had been holding his breath and released it quickly. "Since you've been gone, Barak brought word to the king of unauthorized meetings going on—meetings being held by Alma."

He was unprepared for Limhi's reaction. The younger man stopped in his tracks and turned to stare at Omer with delight on his face.

"Alma? He's still alive? Omer, that is good news." Then he stiffened. "But you have more to share."

Omer nodded his head. "Yes, lord. The king gave Barak orders to take Gideon and his men and capture Alma and those that he claimed have been speaking against him. They left three days ago."

The two men walked silently and slowly between the flower beds. Limhi was the first to speak.

"And so my father is concerned that Barak has

9

failed in this mission for him."

"Yes, lord."

"He is afraid...and with good reason. Omer, he is my father. I am not unaware of those things that he does that are wrong...and yet, he is my father. If Abinadi's words have been shared, if Alma has said more...my father is not safe." Without realizing it, he shredded the red flower he had unconsciously picked.

"Lord Limhi, how much...how did...?"

Limhi laughed quietly. "How much have I known of the words of Abinadi? Come, lord chamberlain, you must know that there are few secrets here. The priests have been concerned—and when I heard their mutterings, I called Gideon to tell me what had happened. I am one of my father's sons, Omer, but that does not mean I have to agree with everything he does."

Omer's ears pricked up. Suddenly he felt that they were being watched, that someone was listening to them.

"My lord, beware! There are dangers everywhere."

Limhi was caught by surprise at the sudden change in tone. He stared at Omer, and then, catching a glimpse of the young man coming toward them, he understood and turned in greeting.

"Ah, so my brother Ammon has come to join us. Greetings, brother."

The two young men stared at each other warily. Although they were almost the same age, there was no love lost between them. Ammon had the dark hair and eyes of his father, the same constant frown, and the beginnings of a paunch that showed too much enjoyment of his father's wine. In contrast, Limhi was fair. His face showed a constant curiosity and concern for things about him, and he looked like a man who had kept himself in shape.

"How was the hunting, my brother?"

Limhi shrugged. "About as well as could be expected."

Ammon sneered. "And what brings you to the garden? I don't recall any interest in our father's flowers before."

Limhi smiled. "New interests can develop, brother. Who knows, one of these days I might discover some new beauty to plant—or some new way to nourish those that are already here."

Ammon's sneer vanished. "Have a care, my brother. I do not intend to lose the throne to anyone."

Limhi's face hardened. "I do not recall speaking about the throne, Ammon."

"Our father might see differently, Limhi." He stared hard at his brother. "I am warning you, brother. Do not interfere with things that are none of your business." There was a long pause. Then Ammon continued with malice in his voice. "You are more like your mother in every way."

He paused, waiting for a response. When Limhi just stood there, saying and doing nothing, Ammon swung on his heel and stomped off.

"Did you know her, Omer?"

Omer shrugged. " A little, Lord Limhi. I know that she did not come here willingly. And once the king grew tired of her, her life here was meaningless."

"I know....I can remember so little about her, Omer. I do remember the stories she used to tell me—stories about how God had protected our people." He paused and looked at Omer. "I don't know—she encouraged me to do what I knew was right, even if everyone else was doing something else."

There was silence for a few minutes until Omer bowed and slowly started moving back through the flowers. Limhi watched. He knew Omer well enough to know that he was a survivor. Right now Omer served Noah—but if it helped him, he would serve Limhi.

Chapter 2

The tension at the court continued to build. It was another three days before the guard sent the all-important message to Omer.

"Lord chamberlain...lord chamberlain...."

Omer turned impatiently. "What is it? Can't you see that I'm busy?"

"Yes, lord. But I was told to give you this message immediately."

Omer sighed. "Well, what is it?"

"There is a cloud of dust to the west. And the watchman on the tower has seen a runner approaching."

"Are you absolutely certain? I must be positive before I take this news to the king."

The messenger nodded his head. "Yes, lord. Absolutely."

Omer smiled "You have done well. Tell your master I will speak with him later."

The messenger made a slight bow. Omer quickly hurried down the hall. As he approached the throne room, he slowed, wondering what kind of condition the king would be in this time. Every time he had found it necessary to enter the presence the last three

13

days, the king had been busy forgetting about his worries by drinking and enjoying the attention of one of the many willing women at court.

He sighed and entered the darkened room. "Most gracious king...."

Noah's grumpy voice responded. "What now, you bringer of gloom?"

"Most gracious king, this time I have good news."

Noah quickly rose to his feet and brushed away the attractive young woman. "Out with you." As he waited for the girl to leave, he pushed aside the jug of wine. "Well, Omer, what now?"

"Lord, I have just received a messenger from the guard. There is a thick cloud of dust to the west, and the watchman on the tower has seen the advance runner."

Noah advanced quickly to Omer. "Are you positive? There is no mistake?"

"No, lord. The messenger is positive there is no mistake."

The king pressed past the little man. "There had better not be."

Omer shivered at the implied threat. He knew that if *anyone* had made a mistake, the results would be blamed on him.

It seemed like hours passed before the runner arrived. He was immediately brought before the king, who was pacing impatiently back and forth.

"Well, what news?"

The runner bowed as low to the floor as he could. "O most gracious king, who had...."

"I said, what news?" The king interrupted the greeting.

As the runner continued to bow to the floor, Omer developed a sinking feeling in the pit of his stomach.

Please let it be good news, he thought, but he knew in his heart it would not be.

"Lord, Gideon and his men are returning."

"I can tell that, you fool! Otherwise you would not be here. But what of Alma? How many of his companions did Gideon bring with him?"

The answer came in a voice so soft it could hardly be heard. "None, lord."

Noah's voice was deceptively soft. "How many?"

The terrified runner repeated his answer. "None, most gracious king."

"None. I assume then that he did at least bring back Alma." The statement fell into thin air. Those members of the court who had hurried to the throne room, ready to rejoice in Alma's downfall, now began to wish they had not been so hasty.

"No, lord. We were unable to find him."

Noah's face began to turn purple, and he shouted, "Unable to find him? I send my best man and a picked troop of soldiers—and you were unable to find him? What happened to everyone?"

The runner began an explanation, but the king was in no mood to listen. "Get out, get out!" As the terrified man backed his way from the royal presence, Noah swung around and shouted, "I will find out what happened! There is some reason—some evil reason behind this failure! Omer...Omer...."

Omer quickly knelt before the king.

"Bring Gideon and Barak to me as soon as they arrive. There is not to be an instant's delay, do you understand? Not an instant!" By the time he ended, Noah was bellowing.

"Yes, lord. They will be brought immediately." Omer also backed away from the royal presence as quickly as possible.

15

He felt it was safer to wait for Barak and Gideon himself than to entrust the message to any of his servants. He knew that if word reached the king of any delay, no matter what the reason, his head would be forfeit. So he spent a long afternoon, pacing back and forth by the gate, constantly checking with the lookout, making certain that he would be the first to greet the soldiers when they returned.

As the afternoon wore on, Limhi joined him. Omer acknowledged his presence, but neither of the two men were interested in talking just for the sake of saying something. The hours passed in silence, until they were finally rewarded with the sight of Gideon and his men entering the palace area.

"Gideon...Gideon...." Omer called, but his voice was drowned out in the sounds of the marching men, and the startled comments from bystanders who saw two men in bonds. Aware of the royal command, Omer quickly worked his way through the crowd. When Gideon spotted him, he ordered his men to stop.

"Lord chamberlain, what brings you here to welcome us back?" Gideon was dusty and tired. He was in no mood to wait any longer than he had to before he could return to his quarters and freshen up.

"I must take you and Lord Barak to the king immediately," panted Omer.

"Now?!" Gideon looked down at himself. "I must have time to clean up. No one approaches the king dressed as I am."

"No, sir. The king insists on seeing you immediately! He has given orders that there is to be no delay whatsoever....Please follow me."

Omer turned back toward the palace, hurrying on his way. Gideon shrugged his shoulders, turned his men over to the second in command, and followed the chamberlain, ordering two of his men to bring Barak and Chemish with them.

When the small group reached the palace Limhi turned and fell in beside them as they entered the cooler hallway and left the buzzing of the crowd outside.

"My lord." Gideon greeted the tall young man beside him.

"Gideon...Lord Barak." There was silence. "I trust you have a good explanation. The king is not pleased with the report from your runner."

There was no spoken response. Gideon just nodded, and Barak continued to stare straight ahead, as he had since their arrival.

Omer bowed before the king and announced, "O most gracious king and lord, Gideon and Barak have just arrived. I have brought them straight to you, as you commanded."

Noah dismissed him with a gesture. Omer scuttled back to the safety of the crowd, while Limhi had already found a place where he could watch the events without his father's eyes on him.

Gideon bowed. "Lord, I am ready to make my report."

"Yes, yes. I only want to know one thing. Why have you not brought Alma and his traitorous followers back to me?"

Gideon faced the king, unafraid. "Lord, I was told that Lord Barak was to be my guide, that he knew where we were to go. We followed his directions, did exactly what he told us to, but Alma had left before we ever arrived."

Noah's face became purple as he turned toward Barak who had not yet said anything.

"And you, Barak...you told me you would not fail. You knew I must have this man back—to force him to recant his words. You knew Alma from his time here—and you failed me."

An ominous silence followed his words.

"Lord king...I did know Alma. I did know of his treasonous activities. You yourself know that I had people watching his every move. My spies told me when and where he was supposed to be. I had every confidence in them, especially Chemish." He glared at the unfortunate man beside him in bonds as he spat out his name. "But...."

Noah came closer to Barak. "But what, Barak? You have failed me too often in this matter."

Barak turned pale. "But, lord, he is gone from your kingdom—he and his traitor friends with him. They will not be back, and their words will be quickly forgotten."

"You fool!" Noah bellowed. "Do you really think that? Too many have heard what he said. Even if no one believes his words, they will still be spoken of...and I will not, must not have that! Yes, Alma is gone, and that is what I wanted. But I wanted to see him—just like I watched Abinadi." The king stopped suddenly and turned his back on Barak. His voice became soft. "Since you did not bring him back—or any of his friends—then you will take his place."

Barak fell to his knees. "Your gracious majesty, I have done my best."

Noah kicked at him. "Your best? Your best has been worthless! How do I know that you are not in league with him, plotting behind my back! No, Barak, I no longer trust you."

Barak groveled. "Please, most gracious king. I beg for one more chance."

Noah sneered. "You've had your last chance, Barak. Remove him to the courtyard and prepare for the sentence to be passed upon him. And take Chemish with him."

Chemish screamed, "No, lord. I am a loyal subject! Alma...."

The king interrupted. "No more! Barak has been one of my priests long enough to know the penalty for failure! And you...you have failed me as well." He turned to the two soldiers holding the men. "Out with them! I will have my vengeance!"

Gideon bowed and left. Barak walked stiffly out of the room, but Chemish had to be dragged. As the procession went down the hallway, those still in the throne room could hear Barak pleading for mercy, and Chemish screaming unintelligible words. Omer felt sick. But I should be grateful that is not my fate, he thought to himself.

No one moved, each person afraid to draw the king's attention to himself. Noah glared around. "Remember, that is the fate of those who fail me...and those who listen to treason." He left the room, taking with him Ammon, who had been standing closely behind him.

Chapter 3

Two years later, Limhi was startled to hear Omer calling him at the entrance to his chambers. There was obvious terror in his voice.

"Lord Limhi...Lord Limhi."

As he moved quickly to greet the little man, Limhi noticed that the chamberlain's clothing was askew. This alone indicated that there was indeed something terribly wrong, for Omer, despite his smallness, was quite vain of his appearance.

"What is it, Omer?"

"Lord Limhi," he panted, "there is mutiny among the soldiers."

"What?!" Limhi was truly astonished. The king's soldiers were well paid; they were the last people he would have expected to raise arms against Noah. "Have you told the king?"

"No, my lord." The chamberlain lowered his head in embarrassment and fear. "I had hoped that you...." His voice trailed off.

"Who is leading this rebellion?" Limhi's voice was sharp.

"I do not know, sir."

Studying the chamberlain, Limhi felt certain that

the man was lying. But there was no way he could prove it. He sighed and turned his back.

"So, what is it you want me to do?"

"Lord, I had hoped that you would talk to the men. They respect you, sir."

Limhi was certin he knew who the leader was. Omer would not have approached him otherwise.

"Very well, Omer. Let's go."

Omer's voice squeaked in surprise. "Me too?"

Limhi nodded. "Of course, chamberlain." There was dark humor in his next words. "You will want to be able to make a full report to my father—and Ammon—if necessary, won't you?"

He did not wait for an answer but left his chambers and hurried through the halls to the barracks. There had been reports of unrest and arguments before, but they had not come this close to the palace. Ever since Alma and his followers had escaped Noah's wrath, the people had been uneasy.

Limhi thought about the reports he had seen—secret reports. Some people had been meeting secretly to plan against his father; others had been meeting to plan strategy to defend him. He shook his head and quickened his step. He knew that there were also arguments in the palace among his brothers over who was to succeed his father as king as well, but so far he had managed to stay clear of them. It looked like this time, though, he was going to be involved, whether he liked it or not.

As he neared the soldiers' quarters, Limhi was surprised to hear Noah's voice being raised. He could not distinguish the words, but he could hear the anger. He smiled wryly as he looked behind him and saw Omer, terrified that the king had already discovered the mutiny.

Noah's voice became clearer. "Who do you trust? I have given you everything you needed or wanted."

"Everything but freedom!" Limhi nodded to himself, recognizing Gideon's voice. He had been certain he was the leader of the rebellion the minute Omer had asked him to come talk, since the two men were friends. But now it appeared that matters were out of his hands.

As they entered the soldiers' quarters, Omer lagged further and further behind. Limhi knew that the chamberlain was terrified to see the king, certain that he would be punished for not having seen the mutiny arising and for not having reported it to the king. It would be in his best interests to stay as much out of Noah's sight as possible.

Limhi knew that he, too, would be wiser to stay out of sight. But curiosity drove him on.

He entered the room and was surprised to see such a large crowd of men. Some he recognized as being under Gideon's command. But there were many he did not remember, and he wondered briefly what had caused them all to band together. Then his attention was drawn back to the confrontation.

The contrast between the two men was startling. Noah was ornately dressed, but his clothes were askew and did not fit him as well as they had. He was not fat, but it was obvious that his body was showing the effects of the strong drink and rich food that he loved. His face was red with anger, and he was glaring at the soldier.

Gideon wore the simple clothes of a soldier, and he showed the fitness of a man who knew that his body was an important weapon. Although he, too, was angry, his anger was under control, and he faced the king in defiance.

"Your majesty, you know that I have served you faithfully for many years. I have obeyed your many orders—I did not complain when you ordered me to remove from the palace all the priests that your father had consecrated. Nor did I complain when you ordered me to kill Abinadi—or sent me out to look for Alma. But I have come to recognize how much of the evil in our kingdom comes from you."

Noah now lost his temper completely. "From me? You dare to slander me, your king?" Seeming to forget where he was, he shrieked, "Arrest this man!"

No one moved.

"No one here will follow your commands, majesty," Gideon answered. "These men follow me."

"You traitor!" Noah turned in anger and confusion.

Limhi watched with surprise and horror as Gideon drew his sword and advanced on the king.

"Stand and fight, sir," he said. "I can no longer follow an evil ruler. Either I die or you do."

Noah glared at him in astonishment. "You forget yourself, Gideon. I am the king."

Gideon shook his head. "I know who you are. Fight or die!"

The king looked around. No one was coming to his rescue. He turned back to face Gideon.

"I am unarmed. Will you kill an unarmed man?"

"No, sire." Gideon made a motion to a soldier near him. The man stepped forward and gave his sword to the king. Noah hefted it, and then faced Gideon.

Limhi continued to watch. He found himself unable to move—unable to rescue either his father or give support to his friend.

Swords clashed. Noah was an accomplished swordsman, although out of practice. Steadily Gideon drove him back, looking for the weakness, waiting for the time to move in and kill.

Suddenly the king stumbled. Everyone in the crowd sensed that the end was near. Gideon continued to press the king, who suddenly turned and ran. The soldiers buzzed in shock, and Gideon, taken by surprise, lowered his sword.

Limhi sagged against a pillar. Although he was pleased that his father had escaped death, he was ashamed that it had been by running. Then he realized that the battle was not over yet. Gideon had followed Noah.

The king knew that there was a tall tower near by, close to the temple that he had built. If I can only get there, he thought, but he could get no further than that. Panting as he ran, he dared not look behind him. He could see the shocked faces of people as he passed, but he could also hear the shouts of the soldiers behind him.

Once he reached the tower, Noah tried to climb the steps quickly. His legs shook, and he sat down to try to regain strength before his enemy arrived. Then he realized that had been a mistake. He could hear Gideon climbing the steps, and he realized that he no longer had the strength to stand, much less to defend himself with the sword.

Desperately he looked around as Gideon came closer. Was there nothing he could do? Suddenly a movement caught his eye, and he looked over the tower toward the land of Shemlon.

"Gideon," he cried out. "Spare me, Gideon."

Gideon made no response except to continue to come closer. Noah motioned in desperation over the edge of the tower.

"Spare me, Gideon, for the Lamanites are upon us,

and they will destroy us. They will destroy my people!"

Gideon stopped. He was certain that the king was lying, but the absolute terror in the king's voice startled him.

"Gideon, look for yourself! The Lamanites are upon us!"

Gideon looked. He was shocked to see the disciplined army approaching. How on earth had they gotten so close without any alarm being sounded? Then his mouth twisted in anger as he remembered—the king had refused to post the number of guards that would have given them the advance warning he had so strongly urged.

King Noah watched anxiously. As he saw Gideon sheath his sword, he sagged in relief.

"Get up," Gideon ordered.

"I am your king!" Noah replied. "You must treat me with respect."

Gideon glared at him with contempt. "Yes, unfortunately you are my king. And for that reason alone I will spare your life. You are concerned only about your own life—not the people—but there must be someone to lead. I have no desire to plunge this people into a civil war. So...."

He turned his back on the king and started back down the tower. After he had gone one or two steps, he stopped, and turned back to King Noah.

"We are not through yet. Remember that."

Chapter 4

Gideon returned to the palace quickly. He found his soldiers roaming around, uncertain of what they should do, and quickly took charge. Order began to be established again, and the men prepared to fight. But Gideon was shocked at what happened next.

King Noah finally had enough strength left to return to the palace. His dignity was in shreds, but he continued to give orders as though nothing had happened.

"Gideon, what are you doing?" was his first question.

"Preparing the men for the battle sir," Gideon replied, perplexed at the question.

"There will be no battle!"

"What?" Gideon was not the only one shocked. But he was the only one who expressed his shock out loud.

Noah's voice rose. "I said there will be no battle! You saw those men out there. We are outnumbered—we will not stand and fight!"

There was a low growl among the men.

"Sir, we may be outnumbered, but we are fighting for our lives and our homes. The Lamanites are simply coming to conquer—we have more...."

"Gideon, I have said there will be no fighting! I am still the king!" Noah glared at the soldier, daring him to disobey.

Gideon held himself rigid. He knew that the king had no desire to go into battle because he was afraid for himself, not because of any fear for his people. But he also knew that he had agreed there needed to be a leader. Slowly his shoulders sagged, and he watched the king smile at his victory.

"Yes, sir. What would you have us do, then?" The sarcasm was heavy, but Noah ignored it.

"Gather the people together and have them flee into the wilderness."

There was definite anger among the soldiers then. Noah ignored it and continued his orders.

"Send runners and warn the people that the Lamanites are almost upon us, and that they are to flee."

Gideon nodded, hating himself for giving in to the king like this. "Yes, sir."

"That is all."

The king turned on his heel then, and left the hall. Gideon silently watched him, and then turned back to his men. He sympathized with the anger he saw on their faces and heard being expressed in low voices, but he knew it had to be stopped.

"Heth, you and Jacob take the west portion of the city. Cohor, you and Jared take the east. Lib, I want you and Moron to take the north, and Sam, you and Zenos take the south. Pass on the king's orders—that there is to be no fighting, and he is ordering the people to flee."

The resentment was strong, but the discipline he had insisted on held. The eight men saluted and then left to do what he had commanded. As soon as they had left, Gideon faced the rest of the soldiers, along with the courtiers who had gathered.

"The rest of you are dismissed. You heard the king. Go home and gather your families and what belongings you can carry easily. You do not have much time—I would suggest that you move fast."

The room emptied quickly. The soldiers left with drooping shoulders—they could not understand why they were not being allowed to do what they knew best. Those members of the court who had been in the room scurried out, thinking frantically of what they could take with them.

Gideon remained, alone. Suddenly he heard a scraping sound and turned quickly. Limhi was staring at him.

"And what of you, my friend? Why have you not left?"

"I have no desire to run, sir. My training is to fight, not run."

Limhi nodded. "I know. But you are needed, Gideon. You must come, too. There must be someone who will be able to give the men the strength and the courage they will need. I am certain we will not all be able to get away—there are too many of us, and the Lamanites are approaching too rapidly."

"We could have defeated them, sir. I know it was possible!"

Limhi slowly started to leave the guardroom. "With you as their leader, I have no doubt of that. But you heard the king's orders." He turned to stare at the older man. "You must not stay here, Gideon."

Gideon stared at Limhi. Limhi held his stare, until the soldier looked away. "I am a soldier, sir. I have been trained to obey orders."

29

Limhi smiled. "Good man. I must leave now, too. Until later...."

"Until later...." Gideon watched as the young man moved rapidly down the halls. He quickly decided his next actions—there was no need for him to return to his home. The few things he needed were in the palace.

As he made his way to the city gate, Gideon shook his head. The streets were in total chaos as the people tried to leave. There were just too many. They would never be able to all get to safety.

Swiftly he wove his way through the crowd, stopping now and then to pick up a child that had fallen, to encourage a woman to leave a bundle she was struggling with. At the gate he was surprised to see Limhi standing there.

"My lord, why are you still here? Don't you realize that you would be a valuable prize to the Lamanites?"

Limhi smiled, a rather twisted smile. "The people need encouragement, Gideon. I would rather not give them the knowledge that I was one of the first ones out, as my father and brothers were. Instead I would let them know that some of us still care for them."

Gideon nodded. But before he could say anything in response, cries of pain and anger could be heard from the far side of the city. He and Limhi looked at each other, knowing that meant that the Lamanites had arrived.

The cries seemed to spur the people on to even greater efforts. Gideon and Limhi worked to get the people through the gate in an orderly fashion. Gideon snatched a moment to look around for the king, sure that he would not see him.

As the crowd lessened, the two men followed them into the wilderness area. They could still hear cries of pain from the city, mixed with cheers of triumph. Gideon's hand went instinctively to his sword, and he turned back briefly. But Limhi touched his shoulder, and after a moment of hesitation, Gideon turned back into the wilderness.

People were scattered all through the forest. Sometimes entire families had sat down, trying to rest the old ones and the children. Gideon and Limhi passed on, encouraging those they saw to move on just a few more steps. They had not gone far when Gideon saw a bedraggled group of men, women, and children. They were carrying the heaviest bundles he had seen yet, and he was certain he recognized some of them from the court.

"Sir, are those not some of your father's people?" Limhi looked up sharply at the question, and then looked in the direction Gideon pointed.

After a moment's hesitation, Limhi nodded. "Those are some of the priests. But...."

Limhi looked around in a questioning manner. Then he walked over to the group. The men looked at him warily, some with resentment on their faces.

"Where are the rest? The king...Ammon...."

A tall, dark-haired man glared at him. "Save yourselves.... That's what he said. Save yourselves!"

Limhi shook his head. "I don't understand."

"The king! When he heard the Lamanites catching up to our people and killing them, he told us to run as fast as we could and save ourselves." Bitterness was evident as he continued to speak. "He didn't care about our families. He was only interested in his own skin. 'Save yourselves.' Well, may he have the kind of luck he deserves!"

Limhi's face reflected the shock he felt. "You mean that he wanted you to leave your families and run?"

"That's what I just said...sire." The sarcasm was evident.

"Who went with him?"

The priest continued to speak. "I don't know for certain. A number of the men left their families and took off running. So did the king himself, your brother Ammon, Omer...I'm not sure who else."

"What about those who were left? Where are the women and children?"

The priest gestured. "Some of them are here. Some of them kept running, trying to catch up. I don't know where they are."

Limhi turned to Gideon. "We must do something, Gideon. I cannot leave all these people to be killed because of the foolishness of my father."

"We cannot stand and fight now, sir. The men are too scattered."

There was a silence, interrupted by one of the young women in the group.

"Lord Limhi, the Lamanites are not that different from us, are they?"

"In what way?" Limhi paused, trying to think of her name.

"I am Sara, sir. I mean...." She paused, blushing. "I mean, sir, am I not attractive?"

Limhi stared. What was she getting at? "Yes, Sara, you are very attractive."

"Then, sir, could my friends and I appeal to the Lamanites?" She looked so trusting and certain of herself that Limhi was touched.

"And just how would you do that?"

Although downcast because of his sternness, she continued stubbornly. "We could go to them, sir...."

Gideon interrupted. "She might have a point, sir. The Lamanites have not yet entered into full-fledged battle. This might be your chance to save the people who remain."

Limhi looked back and forth between Gideon and the girl. "Do you know what you're asking?" he demanded. "Do you realize that these men you're wanting to approach are soldiers—soldiers who have been killing?"

"Yes, my lord. But I would rather die trying to do something rather than just waiting here to be killed."

Several of the other young women nodded their heads in agreement. No one spoke in opposition, although Limhi could see resentment on the faces of some of the priests.

Seeing no alternative, he finally gave in.

"Very well. Gideon, take the girls back toward the city gates."

Chapter 5

Limhi sat gloomily under the tall tree, away from the rest of the people.

"I should never have let Gideon talk me into letting them go," he mused. "They will be killed—or worse!" Suddenly he rose and paced. "How could I be such a fool? I should have ordered Gideon to get a group together and attack!" Then his shoulders sagged. "But the king ordered otherwise—and besides, we are terribly outnumbered."

He paused, listening anxiously for the cries he was sure he would hear. But hearing only the sound of a few birds, he began pacing again.

"Lord, if you are really there, guide me! I do not know which way to turn. I have believed in you—help me know where to go..."

Suddenly there was a rustle in the bushes. Limhi turned sharply, drawing his sword.

"Who's there? Show yourself!"

"My lord."

"Gideon! What news?" Limhi put his sword back in its sheath as the older man appeared. "What of the girls?"

"They are safe, my lord. It is as Sara said—the

soldiers were attracted by the beauty of our young women, especially since they were not caught up in battle."

Limhi sat quickly. "Then the people are safe?"

"Yes, my lord."

"And what are the requirements of the Lamanites? I am certain that they are not granting us safety that easily! They do not have a tradition of mercy!"

Gideon bowed. "Lord, the conditions are to be placed before you. The Lamanite king wishes me to bring you to him to hear the conditions."

Getting to his feet, Limhi brushed himself off. "Very well. But why me?"

"Because, sire, you are the only member of your family who can be found."

Limhi nodded, and the two men began walking toward the city wall. They had not gone very far when three of the Lamanite soldiers intercepted them.

"You are to come with us!" They were harsh in their language. Gideon was about to protest, but a look from Limhi kept him silent.

"I am Limhi—I wish to see your king."

"You will. He is waiting for you in the city."

The three men set a quick pace. Limhi and Gideon were almost out of breath by the time they reached the palace, where the Lamanite king was waiting.

He stared at the two men. "So, you are the son of the king," he sneered.

Limhi stood straight. "I am Limhi."

"And this?"

"This is Gideon, my commander."

The king laughed. "Some commander! His men just ran as we approached! My men would have stayed and fought to protect their homes!"

Limhi could see Gideon struggle to hold his anger in. "My lord, I have come to discuss the terms you require of us."

The Lamanite king sat down casually on the throne. "Yes, what do I wish of you? I do not need your 'soldiers'!" The men around him laughed. "What do you have that is worth your lives?"

Limhi remained silent. He knew that it was better for the terms to come from the Lamanites. Then he might have a chance of making them better for his people. If *he* offered anything, however, he knew that the Lamanite king would probably increase the demands.

The silence continued. The king looked thoughtfully at the young man. "Well, what can you offer?"

"It is up to you, sir, to tell me."

A couple of the Lamanite soldiers started for their swords at what they perceived as the insolent tone of Limhi's response. But at a gesture from the king, they stopped.

"So, you have spirit—not like the rest of your people. I shall find great pleasure in humbling you, Limhi!"

The king arose. "Now hear my terms. You and your people may live—and in this land—under these conditions. I expect you to deliver King Noah to me. I expect you to give me one half of all you possess—now, and every year!"

Limhi gulped. "My lord, we do not know where the king is. How can we deliver him to you?"

The Lamanite king smiled. "That I leave to you. There is no time limit on when you bring him to me. But he is mine!"

Limhi nodded. "And the rest, sire. My people will have nothing left to work with."

"Do not push me, Limhi!" the king bellowed. "Those are my terms. Either you accept them—or you die!"

There was a tense silence. Then Limhi nodded.

"Very well, my lord. We will accept the terms."

"Fine, fine. Then you will be king of this people, Limhi. I am certain we can work together to our mutual good and satisfaction!" The Lamanite king came down to Limhi and motioned to the throne. "The seat is yours, my lord. Take it and rule in good health!"

The Lamanite king and his soldiers left the room, laughing loudly. Limhi and Gideon stood quietly, waiting until they were the only ones left.

"My lord, how can you do this?" Gideon exploded. "How can you give in to those demands?"

"Do you see that we have a choice?" Limhi retorted. "He made it quite clear that either we do as he says or we all die. If it were just me, I would have no problem. But how can I doom all the rest of my people to death? No, Gideon, I cannot do that. We shall simply have to do the best we can."

After several weeks, the city returned somewhat to normal. Limhi was installed as king and presented the first payment of tribute to the Lamanites sent to collect it. There was some grumbling, but most of the people were so happy to be alive that the collection went easily.

Gideon was still unhappy about the decisions that had been made and was again preparing to marshall his arguments.

"Gideon, I have heard your complaints. I agree with you that the situation is not good—but what would you have me do?"

Gideon remained silent.

"I have a task for you, old friend." Gideon looked at the king sharply. "And this is important. I wish you to pick trusted men—men who will keep secrets."

"Yes, Lord Limhi. How many do you need?"

Limhi pulled at his lip. "I don't know, Gideon. I want you to send them out in search parties. They must be large enough that they can carry enough supplies to survive—but they must be small enough that they can get away unnoticed."

Gideon began to stir with excitement. "To where, sir?"

"I don't know that, either. The Lamanite king has ordered us to turn my father over to him. I know that he did much wrong—but he is still my father, Gideon. I would like you to send the men out to search for him—but secretly, so the Lamanites do not hear of it."

"And then what? What happens when we find him?"

Limhi stopped and stared into space. "I don't know, Gideon. If you find him, bring him back as quickly and quietly as you can. I will try to think of something."

"Lord, they will leave as soon as possible."

Limhi turned to look at him. "Remember, Gideon. They must be picked men, and the mission must be secret."

Gideon nodded as he turned to the barracks. He knew exactly who he was going to pick.

Three weeks passed. Limhi did not question Gideon orally, but Gideon could see the questions in his eyes each time the king looked at him. As much as he was able to, he ignored the king. He knew that others at the court resented his behavior, but he also knew that the king accepted his actions.

Finally the day came when he approached the king. "My lord, I have a report."

Limhi sagged in relief. But as he continued to search Gideon's face, he drew his shoulders up, prepared for bad news.

"Where?"

"I think it would be best to hear it here, my lord, with the members of the court present."

Limhi nodded. "Bring them in, then, Gideon."

Gideon made a small motion. The group of picked soldiers entered, along with many other men Limhi knew well. He recognized Omer as well as some of the other court officials he had known for years.

Limhi noticed that most of them averted their faces as much as they dared. Only one looked straight at him, and Limhi motioned him forward.

"Yes, my lord." There was respect in this man's attitude but no fear. Limhi liked that.

"Your name is Seth, is it not?"

"Yes, my lord."

Limhi sat heavily. "Very well, Seth, what report can you give me?"

Seth bowed. "My lord, as you know, many of us ran with your father, the king, leaving our wives and children behind." Ignoring the angry mutterings, he continued. "We hid out in the wilderness, afraid, because we did not know what would happen to us. We were afraid of being killed. But a few days ago, those of us who are here decided to return and see what had happened to our wives and children. If the Lamanites had killed them, we were determined to avenge them, even if it meant that we would also die in the attempt."

Someone in the crowd called out, "Why didn't you

stay with them if you were so concerned?" There were mutterings of agreement from others, which died away quickly as Limhi glanced around.

"Continue, Seth."

"My lord. I regret that I did not stay with my wife and children. I have had time to think, and doubt that I would react the same way again. As I said, though, we were determined to return. But your father...." Seth paused, looking warily at Limhi.

Then he continued. "The king, though, commanded us not to return. We tried to argue with him, but he was adamant that none of us should return for fear of what would happen."

As he paused again, Limhi noticed that other members of the group were now looking down, shuffling their feet, and giving every indication that they would definitely rather be somewhere else. He ordered Seth to continue, sure that he knew what was to come.

"My lord...."

"There will be no retribution, Seth. There has been enough killing."

"Yes, my lord." There was a long pause as Seth gathered his thoughts. "When the king refused to allow us to return, several of us became angry." He looked straight at Limhi. "We took him, sir, and burned him at the stake."

Limhi barely heard the gasps of shock and anger that arose around him. He was sure that his father was dead, but he had not dreamed that Noah would die this way. He felt dizzy but pressed his fingernails into the palms of his hands, commanding himself not to faint.

"And what of his priests, Seth? I notice that they are not with you."

41

"No, my lord. They escaped from us and went deeper into the wilderness."

Limhi sat in thought. He remembered the good times he had had with his father—but he also remembered the cruelty he had become aware of as he grew up. As he looked up, he could see the fear in the men's faces as they waited to see how he would react.

"Go to your homes—all of you. There has been enough suffering among this people. Return to your wives and children."

The men who had been members of his father's court bowed and left. Limhi waved away the rest of his court, and they also left, all but Gideon.

Gideon approached his king. "My lord," he began gently.

"No, Gideon, not now. I need time to think."

But Gideon refused to be dismissed. "Yes, my lord. But there is something you need to remember as you think."

Limhi raised his head and looked at his commander. "What is it, Gideon?"

"My lord, you have my sympathy on the death of your father. But as Abinadi was dying...."

"What does Abinadi have to do with us at this time, Gideon?" Limhi's voice was flat.

"You were not there, sir. But in his last words, he said that many would suffer death by fire and that we would have all kinds of diseases and be struck and driven to and fro—because God would take vengeance on those who destroy his people."

"And so it starts...." Limhi dropped his face into his hands. Quietly Gideon left the chamber.

Chapter 6

Two years passed. Although the people of Limhi did not enjoy having the Lamanite guards posted in their land, they did manage to get along with them. Gradually they began to forget the horrors of the previous wars. As the people worked hard, they were able to grow enough to supply themselves after the tribute was collected for the Lamanites. They were not as wealthy as before, but they were survivors.

Limhi spent time every day in the watch tower. Omer, who was chamberlain again, one day dared to ask what many in the court wondered.

"My lord, what are you looking for? Every day you go up there. Why?"

Limhi smiled and looked around. "I don't know that I am especially looking for anything. However, I want to be prepared for everything."

Omer continued. "But, my lord, the Lamanites have promised to leave us in peace as long as we pay the tribute."

Limhi's smile twisted. "And we have paid it. I don't know, Omer. I just have to be there every day."

Gideon and Seth were also in the throne room that day. Gideon shook his head as he looked around the room. "I don't understand it, Seth. How can these people be so trusting?"

"They are not as naive as you think, Gideon," Seth replied. "They just want to forget the past. They have managed to convince themselves that everything will be fine..." His voice trailed off.

"And what about you? Do you think that everything will be fine as long as we continue to pay our tribute?"

Seth shook his head. "When have we been left in peace for very long? We have not really had peace for years, Gideon. Either we have had problems among ourselves or we have been fighting outside forces. No, Gideon, I think we need to be prepared."

Their conversation ended as Limhi prepared to leave and go up the tower. Spotting Gideon, he motioned to him to attend him.

Gideon knew the tower well. On this day, he was reminded of the last time King Noah had climbed it—the day he left in such unmajestic haste. As was Limhi's custom, when he reached the top, he slowly circled to look in each direction, taking special care to look toward the border. Suddenly Gideon saw him stiffen.

"My lord?"

"Gideon, come here and tell me what you see."

Startled by the passion in the king's voice, Gideon hurried to his side. Carefully he looked in the direction the king was pointing. At first he saw nothing. Then he caught his breath.

"Oh no." He gasped almost without thinking.

"You see it, too?" The king spoke calmly.

"Yes, sir." Gideon felt his stomach muscles tense. In the back of his mind he had been expecting the Lamanites to come against them some day, but "some day" had always been a long way off.

"They are still far off, Gideon. We have time to arrange an ambush. Go and prepare, Gideon. But be careful. If their king has come with them, I want him taken alive. I must know why they have come."

Gideon nodded, his mind whirling with plans, people and places. Quickly he and the king left the tower and returned to the palace, where they separated.

Limhi summoned Omer and curtly commanded him to bring Seth, who had become the only member of Noah's court that the king trusted. When the younger man appeared, Limhi studied him carefully.

"Seth, you have been in charge of collecting the tribute."

"Yes, lord."

"Have there been any problems with it?"

Seth looked mildly puzzled as he answered. "No, lord. The people have grumbled as usual, but it has all been collected and sent to the Lamanites."

"You are certain of that?"

Limhi could tell that his question annoyed Seth, but he answered calmly. "Yes, my lord, I am certain. I can bring the books for you to see if you desire."

There was silence for a long moment as the king stared directly at Seth. The two men looked at each other, and it was the king who turned away first.

"No, Seth...if you are certain, then it has been done."

"My lord...." Seth was uncertain.

"Yes?"

"My lord, could you tell me why?" Limhi could hear some of the other courtiers in the room gasp at the unexpected question. He smiled, knowing they expected an outburst of rage like his father would have done.

45

"I did not really doubt you, Seth. I had just hoped there was a simple reason for the Lamanites to march upon us." Limhi watched as the import of what he had just said dawned upon all those in the room. A wild buzzing broke out, and he could hear the panic begin to build.

"There is nothing to be alarmed about. They are far enough off that Gideon is arranging to meet them—on our terms." The room emptied quickly after that. A few of the men went to help Gideon in any way they could, but Limhi knew that most of them would be going to find hiding places for their valuables—and themselves.

For his part, Gideon was busy with his soldiers. They had not had much to do for the past two years, but he had kept them busy with as much training as he could under the eyes of the Lamanites. There were still some men who were green and untrained, but many of his men had been with him for years and could be trusted, despite their forced inactivity.

Quickly he called his captains to him. They held council as he outlined the king's request.

"Our best chance is to set up an ambush. We are badly outnumbered, but if we can catch them by surprise, we may startle them so much that they will waver for a short time. Then we must press our advantage. Otherwise our conditions will become much worse."

"Where do you want us, Gideon?" It was Pagag who raised the question. Gideon looked around the circle.

"I want your suggestions first. I have an idea, but I want to hear your advice."

There was silence as the men thought about the area where they would be fighting. Mentally each of them placed troops in the best location for an ambush. Gideon watched them, and when he was sure they had had time to think, he started questioning.

"Pagag, where would you place your men?"

As Pagag explained his strategy, the others nodded agreement. Corom jumped in with a comment as Pagag finished, and then the others quickly made their suggestions. Gideon listened for a few minutes, and finally held up his hand for silence.

"You have good suggestions. Some of them we do not have time to implement, but here is what we will do." Quickly he explained his plan. "Are there any questions? Any final comments?" The men were silent.

"Then go and place your men." As the circle of men started to break up, Gideon issued one last warning. "Remember, the king must be taken alive."

Gideon found Limhi pacing back and forth in the throne room.

"My lord, my men are taking their places even as we speak."

"Good, Gideon. Take runners with you. I will watch from the tower."

Gideon nodded his approval. As he turned to leave, Limhi called to him again.

"Gideon, remember...the king must be taken alive. I *must* know why they have come to war against us." His voice dropped. "Then perhaps I can offer my people some protection."

The Lamanites came on, unafraid, with no attempt to hide. There was shouting and cheering as they came within sight of the town. Limhi could not repress a slight shudder as he saw them with their war decorations and weapons. He knew the women and children would be terrified.

"Oh, God, please protect my people...." His voice trailed away for a moment, and then he continued. "We have tried to do what is right. Be with Gideon and help him to succeed."

As the Lamanites drew closer, the shouting and cheering stopped. They became uneasy when they realized there were no soldiers on the wall and none leaving the city gate. Limhi watched as their commanders halted and met together. It became obvious that their decision was to continue their attack, even if it meant fighting house-to-house.

Slowly the Lamanites started forward again. But they were startled as one of Gideon's captains attacked from behind. There was a brief moment of panic, and then the commanders had control of their men again, turning them to fight. Just as it seemed that they were going to drive off the Nephites, Pagag attacked with his men from the right. Again there was that brief moment of panic, and then a settling down to battle.

Limhi watched intently. The Lamanites responded in surprise as small groups attacked them from every side. They did not know which way to turn, and soon Limhi observed that the Lamanites seemed to be trying to pull back.

Then Limhi noticed four or five men who had separated from the main battle, with one person running before them. He hurried down from the tower and back to the palace.

The runner entered the throne room, bowed quickly, and then spoke. "My lord, we have found the king of the Lamanites. He had been left for dead by his people, and we have brought him to you. Now let us kill him."

"No, you must not kill him. Have Gideon bring him

here so that I can see him and question him."

Obviously disappointed, the man left, returning quickly with Gideon and the others.

"My lord," Gideon spoke. "Here is the man you requested us to bring you. He was left for dead by his people, but we have bound his wounds." He gestured to the man who was being carried on a makeshift litter.

Limhi approached the king, who watched him warily, obviously expecting the worst.

"Why have you brought your people to war against mine?"

The wounded man struggled to raise himself to a sitting position, but Limhi continued.

"My people have not broken the oath that we made to you. We have sent our tribute, we have supported your soldiers. Why have you broken your part of the agreement?"

Despite his obvious pain, anger flared in the eyes of the Lamanite king.

"I will agree—you have continued to pay your tribute. But your people have kidnapped the daughters of my people! For this cause we have come to war against you."

Limhi was surprised. "I have heard nothing about this." He turned to Omer, who was watching the action intently. "Omer, order a search to be made among my people. Whoever has been involved in this shall surely die."

As Omer left, another runner quickly entered the room and spoke to Gideon. Gideon listened, nodded, and then stepped forward.

"My lord," he began. "This is not the fault of your people."

Limhi and the Lamanite king both turned toward him. But Limhi was the first to speak.

"What do you mean, Gideon?"

"Do you not remember the priests of your father, sir? They are still in the wilderness somewhere, afraid to come home. Surely they are the ones who have kidnapped these women."

Limhi turned away and sat heavily on his throne. Gideon stepped forward, continuing to speak.

"Sir, we must tell the king those things we know so that he can tell his people. They are coming to attack us again, and they outnumber us." Gesturing toward the Lamanite king in the litter, he continued. "Unless the king has them make peace with us, we will surely die. This is the fulfillment of what Abinadi prophesied."

There was silence for a few moments, and then Gideon spoke again. "My lord, let us make peace with the king, and fulfill the terms of the agreement we have made. Surely it is better to live in bondage than for all to lose their lives! We must stop the shedding of blood among our people."

Slowly Limhi nodded. "You are right, Gideon. This must be stopped." He turned toward the king who had laid back in the litter.

"My lord king, it is not my people who have broken the oath. When you attacked us before, when I agreed to your terms, there were some who were not part of that agreement—my father and his priests. I have had Gideon looking for all of them, but so far without success."

The Lamanite king sounded cynical. "No success at all?"

"No, lord, not completely. Seth, tell the king what you know."

Seth was surprised that Limhi had even been aware that he had come in. But he stepped forward, telling the Lamanite king of the events that led to Noah's death by fire.

Then Limhi continued. "There has been no sign of the priests, but they must be the ones who have stolen your daughters." He smiled slightly. "They belong to no one's group...afraid to come back here, but not willing to join you. We will keep looking for them, but this I swear to you. As soon as they are found, we will tell you and return your daughters to your people."

The Lamanite king listened. After Limhi finished, there was silence again as he considered all that he had been told. Finally he nodded.

"Very well. Let us go and meet my people without arms. I swear to you that my people will not kill yours."

A sigh of relief could be heard. Gideon directed the soldiers to carefully pick up the litter, while Limhi commanded everyone else to remain behind. Slowly the small procession left the city gates.

Both armies were preparing to battle again. But all preparations stopped at the sight of the small group. The Lamanite king ordered the soldiers to help him stand, and then commanded his captains to approach him.

At a command from him, Limhi and Gideon repeated the story they had already shared. It was obvious that not everyone believed them, but the Lamanite king demanded obedience.

"I have promised that we will not kill them—and they, in good faith, have promised to try to help find our daughters. So, you are to regroup and we will return to our own land."

There was rebellion on the faces of several of the Lamanite leaders, but no one dared defy their king.

Limhi also ordered Gideon to withdraw his troops.

"Yes, lord, it shall be done."

It was not easy to completely disengage the soldiers, but eventually the task was accomplished. The Lamanite king, in his litter, was given over to the care of his own men. Limhi and Gideon returned to the watchtower to observe the withdrawal.

"I'm afraid we have not seen the last of them, Gideon," Limhi said thoughtfully.

"Nor I, sir...although they did promise not to kill us." Gideon responded.

Limhi smiled ruefully. "There are still many things the king did not promise, though." He turned to leave the tower. "I fear we have many dark days ahead of us."

Chapter 7

"No, Seth, I will not go back to the king again." Gideon stood up and began pacing back and forth.

"But, Gideon..."

With emphatic gestures, Gideon repeated his answer. "No, Seth, I will not go back." He turned to face the younger man. "If I thought we had any chance of success—any chance at all, I would ask permission to lead the army again. But we have tried three times to escape." He slumped to the ground. "I am tired of hearing the cries of the people. There are too many widows and orphans."

Although Seth's face showed his disappointment, he knew better than to push Gideon. He joined him under the tree that was just inside the city walls—one of the few places where they could hold a private discussion.

"Then what are we to do?"

Gideon shrugged his shoulders. "I don't know for sure. All I can suggest is that we bow to our situation right now. Sometime a chance will come—but not now." He turned to look Seth straight in the eyes. "We cannot even capture the priests of Noah—if we could do that, we might be able to bargain with the

Lamanites. I have no answers any more, Seth."

The two men sat quietly, resting in the sun. They were both lost in their private thoughts, until they heard cries for help. Seth jumped up first, with Gideon following more slowly.

"Softly, Seth. We must see what is happening."

Cautiously the two men walked toward the source of the cries. Suddenly Gideon stopped abruptly.

"There, Seth."

Gideon's face set in anger as he saw ten of the Lamanite soldiers surrounding a young mother and her two young children. They were removing their heavy packs and loading them onto the three Nephites. The younger child, only four years old, could just barely hold one of the packs, while the other child, an eight-year-old, was struggling to hold two of them. The other seven packs were being piled onto the woman, who was about to fall.

"Come on, woman, carry these to our rooms!" As the poor woman attempted to take a step, the soldiers roared with laughter. The little boy began to cry, and tried to grab hold of his mother.

"Here, you, keep hold of that pack! Come on, brat!" The little boy looked around in astonishment at the harsh tone and made a valiant effort to lift the heavy burden. It was far too heavy for him, however, and even though his sister tried to help, she was burdened with her two packs. The face of the soldier who had spoken twisted in rage, and he slapped the face of the young boy.

Gideon stepped forward just in time to stop Seth from charging the soldiers. Although he was trembling with rage, Gideon said nothing. He went straight to the little family group, took four of the packs from the woman, and smiled in encouragement at them. Seth followed, taking the packs from the children, and one more from the woman.

The soldiers were astonished to see the two men appear and were silent for a moment. Then one of them recognized Gideon and began taunting him.

"So—the great war hero has stooped to carrying women's burdens, has he?"

The other soldiers laughed and joined in the taunting. Seth felt his muscles tighten, and he clenched his fists. But Gideon, although his face turned red, said nothing. He simply turned and started up the street.

"How do you know where we're going, great one?"

Gideon stopped. Turning to face the speaker, he quietly responded. "You are going to your quarters, are you not?"

It was obvious the soldier had been hoping for a sharp retort, one that would give him justification for treating Gideon badly. But the civility and submission in Gideon's voice permitted the soldier only to nod. The little group became quiet, as Gideon and Seth carried the soldiers' packs to their quarters.

As quickly as possible, the Nephites left. Gideon escorted the woman and her children to their home and left them with a warning.

"Be careful when you go out. Go out only with others in a group—that way you might have better protection."

She smiled wearily. "Thank you, Gideon."

As the two men left her home, Gideon was quiet, although he set a quick pace toward the palace. "Now what, Gideon?"

"We must see the king, Seth."

Seth was astonished. "But I thought you said you would not go to him again."

Impatiently Gideon answered. "Not for permission to go to war again. But we must do something to protect our people—and I am not certain what."

At the palace, Gideon was stopped briefly by Omer.

"I'm sorry, Lord Gideon. But the king has given no one permission to intrude."

"Omer, get out of my way! I will put up with you and your ways many times—but not when it affects the people!"

The litle man ineffectually tried to stop Gideon, but the older, larger man just brushed right by him. Omer turned to Seth for help.

"Sire, the king will be most unhappy!"

Seth just shrugged his shoulders.

"Sorry, Omer. Nothing is going to stop Gideon when he is doing what he is convinced is right. I'm afraid you are just out of luck."

Omer continued to moan and wring his hands as he watched Gideon disappear into the king's private quarters.

Limhi looked up as Gideon entered. It was obvious he was prepared to immediately respond angrily, but Gideon spoke first.

"My lord...."

"What are you doing here, Gideon? I have given orders that I am not to be disturbed today."

"I know, my lord."

The king arose. "You know? And yet you came anyway? I could have you killed for that, you know."

Gideon nodded. "You could—but you will not."

Limhi shook his head in disbelief. "You are awfully certain of yourself, my friend. Why shouldn't I?"

"Because you still need me—and because you are not like your father, who killed on a whim."

The king thrust a curtain aside and looked outside. He spoke quietly.

"You are right, Gideon. I do still need you. There are so few people I can really trust." Turning with a smile, he continued. "And you will always tell me the truth, even when I would rather not hear it. So now what?"

"My lord, you know I have come to you before for permission to lead the people in battle against the Lamanites..."

Limhi shook his head. "Not again, Gideon. We have lost too many people already."

Gideon nodded in agreement. "That is not why I have come, lord. But we must do something to protect our people." Quietly he recounted what had happened earlier in the day.

The king listened, his face growing darker.

"This is intolerable, Gideon! These are innocent women and children!"

The two friends were quiet for a moment. Then the king continued. "But I am afraid that the Lamanites are within their rights." He smiled. "After all, their king did promise that they would not kill us—but he said nothing about putting heavy burdens upon us."

Gideon sat heavily. "Lord, I am afraid that we are in for more difficult times. Abinadi prophesied, just before he died, that we would be struck on every side and be driven to and fro. I am afraid that this is that time."

"Then what are we to do, Gideon?"

There was silence as the two men thought. Finally Gideon shrugged his shoulders.

"My lord, I do not see that we have much choice. We must encourage the people to stay in groups as much as possible that will still allow us to raise our crops and take care of our flocks. The children must be kept together, under the protection of the older boys, so that they will be at least somewhat protected from the Lamanites."

Limhi looked encouraged. "Yes, and we must begin to take care of the women and children. Every man must give a certain percentage of his goods—at least from what's left over after we give our tribute to the Lamanites—to help keep our people from starvation."

Gideon nodded. "There will be some who will not like that, sire."

Limhi shrugged angrily. "That is too bad. There is no one who can say that he is any better than any one else in our kingdom. We are in this together—we will work together to help each other." He turned his back on Gideon. "Perhaps if we had been more willing to listen to Abinadi and Alma and the others, this would not have happened to us."

"Sire, I can offer only two other suggestions." Anxiously, Gideon waited for the king's response. "We must spend time in prayer. Perhaps if we call upon God all the time, he will hear us."

Limhi nodded. "I hope so. Perhaps he will forgive our sins.... And your other suggestion?"

"You, sir. You must constantly keep guards with you, sire, especially if you go outside the walls of the city. I do not trust the Lamanites."

Gideon expected the king to be angry. But to his surprise, Limhi thoughtfully weighed the suggestion and found it good.

"Yes, Gideon, I think you are right. And I expect you to train and assign the guards—your trusted men."

The weeks passed, and the recommendations were

put into effect. No one went anywhere unless in a group; even the children quickly learned. As Gideon walked through the streets, he noted with satisfaction that while the people were still being made to carry heavy burdens, at least the weaker ones were given more help by being in groups.

After six months Gideon was summoned to the palace and shown directly to the king's private quarters.

Limhi turned to greet him. "Old friend, I need your advice."

Gideon carefully greeted the king. "How may I help you, sire?"

"I want a report on how things are going. You are my trusted eyes and ears, Gideon. I get reports from other members of my court, but I am not really certain how far they can be trusted—or how much they are letting themselves be deceived."

"In what way?"

Limhi sat heavily. "The burdens being placed on my people. Are they still as heavy as they were?"

Gideon shook his head. "The Lamanites still use every excuse they can find to load our people down—but the burdens do not seem as heavy. I do not know if it is because there are more to share the load, or...." He paused.

"Or what, Gideon?"

"Or if the Lord is finally hearing our prayers. Whatever the reason, sir, we are coping better with the situation."

"And what about the food? I have ordered the arrangements we talked about, to help feed the widows and orphans. The reports I receive say that it is going well."

Gideon smiled. "It is going very well, my lord. There has been little grumbling. And our crops are increasing, so that even with what we have to pay the Lamanites, there is still enough and to spare. No one is going hungry."

"Praise God!" Limhi's shoulders sagged with relief. "I had thought that perhaps Omer and the others were just telling me what they thought I wanted to hear."

"No, sire." Gideon shook his head. "I hate to say it, but it may be that this experience is providing a means for us to return to an awareness of our God." His voice fell. "I just wish there was someone here who could teach us more like Abinadi could have."

Limhi nodded. "The day will come, Gideon, I am sure of it."

Chapter 8

"Gideon, gather your guards. I am going to go outside the walls."

Gideon looked up, startled. He was one of many in the room. There had been no indications of anything unusual until the king spoke.

"When, sir?"

Limhi responded impatiently. "As soon as you get your men together, Gideon."

The older man bowed. "Yes, sir."

Quickly he left the room, heading to the barracks, muttering under his breath. "Of all the days to be impatient."

There were several soldiers lounging around when he arrived. Gideon looked around, spotted one of the men he had put in charge of a guard detail. He sighed to himself—a fine time for one of the younger men to be on duty!

"Lammonihah, get your detail together—immediately!"

"Yes, sir."

"And meet me at the palace gate."

Immediately there was a bustle of activity in the room. Gideon waited to be certain that all was in order. Then he quickly returned to his room to gather the equipment he felt was necessary.

"The men are ready, sire."

Limhi nodded. He broke off his conversation and left. Gideon hurried to catch up with him, trying to figure out what was going on.

"Sire, where do you want to go? Or do?"

Without slowing down, Limhi turned to smile. "I'm just tired of being cooped up, Gideon. It's time to stretch my legs—and time to give the guards some exercise. I plan to go outside the walls and see what's going on."

"But sir."

"No, Gideon, I want no complaints. It's a beautiful day, and I intend to take full advantage of it." The king looked around. "I know I am ruler—but only because the Lamanites wish me to be. I cannot protect my people as I would wish. Have you never been frustrated, Gideon?"

Gideon nodded. As the small group of men walked quickly through the streets, he thought of all the frustrations he had felt since the Lamanites had come in as the conquerors. Primary among them was the fact that he still had not been able to capture the priests of Noah, those men who had caused so many problems for the people. Despite all his attempts and all the patrols he had sent out, the only signs of the priests had come from the capture of the Lamanite girls and the thefts of food stores. That really made him angry. There was now enough for the people after giving the Lamanites their tribute, but Gideon had no desire to give any extra to that group of men!

Quickly he came back to the present, recognizing that they were almost to the city wall.

"Lammonihah, make absolutely certain that your

men are on their guard," he ordered.

"Yes, sir," Lammonihah responded. Turning to his men, he began to separate them into smaller groups. Gideon watched, ready to make changes if necessary to protect the king. But as he listened, he nodded his head in agreement. Although he was young, Lammonihah was doing a good job of sending small patrol groups out ahead while still leaving a large enough group to allow them to protect the king well.

Limhi did not seem to notice all the arrangements being made, but Gideon knew that was not so. Limhi was aware of every move that was being made, and that became obvious in his comment as he turned to Gideon.

"Well, old friend, is it safe now for us to move ahead?"

Gideon grimaced. "As safe as it can be, my lord."

Limhi nodded. "Then let's go. I am anxious to see for myself—not just hear reports."

Limhi was more thoughtful in his walking now. He kept a careful watch about him, stopping periodically. Gideon was also especially alert. He was not anxious to have trouble break out outside the wall—and then to have to try to explain that to their Lamanite overlords!

But everything remained quiet. There was no one else outside the walls but them. Finally Limhi seemed to be satisfied and prepared to turn back.

"All does seem quiet, Gideon. I am pleased with your attention to detail."

"Thank you, sire." Gideon smiled. "I just wish we were able to capture those priests of your father. Then maybe we could get the Lamanites off our back!"

Limhi nodded soberly. "It would certainly give us

something to bargain with. Maybe one of these days...."

Gideon never knew how Limhi was going to complete that sentence. Just then there came a call from one of the scout patrols.

"Sir...my lord...."

"Stay here, my lord!" As he ran ahead, Gideon was surprised to see the patrol returning with four men bound in front of them. He turned to Lammonihah, who had come up behind him. "Your men have done well!"

The two groups stopped, facing each other. Gideon took charge unconsciously. "Where did you find them?"

The young soldier saluted. "We were patrolling over the hill, like Lammonihah ordered. And these four men were coming out of the forest. We ordered them to stop." He paused for a moment, and when he continued, he sounded puzzled. "They did, sir. Our orders were to capture anyone we found out here."

Gideon nodded. "You did well. The only people we could expect to find out here are troublemakers. Take them back and put them in prison. The king will want to talk to them."

He turned his back on them, preparing to return to the king. But just before he left, Lammonihah caught his attention.

"Are there any special orders, sir?"

"What? Oh, no. Make certain they are given enough food and water, but no one is to see them. We will find out soon enough where the rest of the priests are."

Lammonihah nodded. Quickly he gave orders, and the patrol headed back toward the city.

As Gideon returned to the king, he ordered the rest

of the soldiers to fall in and form a protective square. Limhi looked startled.

"What has happened, Gideon?"

"Sir, we have captured, I believe, some of the priests of your father."

"Where? What did they say?"

"They said nothing, sir. That is what puzzles me."

"Nothing? Are you certain?" Limhi stopped. "They made no protests? Nothing?"

Gideon shook his head. "No, sir."

"That certainly does not sound like the priests I knew!"

The group of men resumed walking back towards the city.

"What have you done with them, Gideon?"

"I ordered Lammonihah to take them on back and put them in prison. They are to be kept isolated until you wish to see them—I thought that might encourage them to give us more information."

Limhi nodded absentmindedly. "You have done well," was his only comment on the return to the city.

Two days passed without any command to Gideon from the king. He was mildly puzzled and wondered what the king intended to do about the men they had captured outside the city walls, but knew that he would hear when Limhi decided it was time.

Finally the summons came. Gideon hurried to the throne room, expecting to find it filled with members of the court. Instead there were only the king, himself, Seth, the chamberlain, and a guard.

As Gideon bowed, the king caught sight of his puzzled expression and chuckled.

"I thought it would be better to find out what is going on without so many gossipers around, my friend." Turning to Omer, Limhi continued, "Tell Lamonnihah to bring them in."

There was no conversation while they waited. Each person in the room was caught up in his own thoughts, wondering what the presence of these men meant. Suddenly the rustle of footsteps was heard, and Lammonihah entered, followed by the four prisoners and their guards.

Omer stood at the door, waiting. "You may leave, Omer,'" Limhi said pointedly. "Seth will be able to do whatever is necessary." With a disappointed expression on his face, Omer left and Seth moved quietly to his place.

The four young men stood quietly, watching. Limhi's next comment caught everyone by surprise. "Release their bonds."

Gideon gasped. "My lord...."

Limhi silenced him with a gesture. "Release their bonds, Lammonihah."

Their bonds were cut. There was silence for a moment as they rubbed their hands. Then the king continued.

"I am Limhi, the son of Noah, who was the son of Zeniff, who came up out of the land of Zarahemla to inherit this land, which was the land of their fathers, and who was made a king by the voice of the people. Now I wish to know why you were so bold as to come near the walls of the city when I was outside them with my guards? This is why you are still alive—that I can ask you. Otherwise I would have caused you to be put to death." After a moment, he continued. "You are permitted to speak."

The four young men looked at each other. Then one of them stepped forward, bowed and stood again. In a calm, assured voice, he began to speak.

"Sir, I am very thankful before God today that I am still alive and am permitted to speak. If you had known who I was, I can assure you that you would not have suffered us to be bound. For I am Ammon, a descendant of Zarahemla, and have come to inquire concerning our brethren whom Zeniff brought out of the land of Zarahemla."

Pandemonium broke out as everyone tried to speak together. Finally Limhi was able to take charge again, and he silenced everyone.

"This causes me great joy! Now I know for certain that my brethren who were in the land of Zarahemla are still alive! Today we will rejoice—and tomorrow my people will rejoice also! We are in bondage to the Lamanites and have to pay grievous taxes." Turning to the four young men, he continued. "These our brothers will deliver us out of our bondage to the Lamanites, and we will be their slaves. It is better that we be slaves to the Nephites than to continue to pay tribute to the king of the Lamanites."

As Limhi paused, the young man who had spoken before made a request.

"Sir, would it be possible to go to the rest of my men and assure them that we are well?"

Limhi was surprised. "Where are they?"

Ammon smiled. "They are hidden in the hill north of Shilom."

"Certainly!" Turning to Lammonihah, the king continued. "Lammonihah, go with these young men. Bring the rest of them straight here so that they can rest and have food and drink."

Lammonihah saluted and then turned to leave. But Limhi continued. "Be careful of the Lamanites, Lammonihah. They must not see the men. May God be with you."

Gideon and the king waited impatiently for the return of the patrol with the rest of the Nephites. They tried to pass some of the time by discussing ways they could use the young men to their advantage in trying to escape but were unable to come up with any new ideas. Finally, growing frustrated, they passed the remainder of the time in silence.

There was a soft, timid knock. All three of the men jumped, and Limhi nodded at Seth to see who was there. Omer bowed as he spoke.

"My lord, Lammonihah and the men you sent out are returning."

"Thank you, Omer," the king replied dryly. As the chamberlain withdrew, Limhi looked at the other two. "It appears we will not be able to keep this secret here. I am concerned, Gideon, about how to keep this news from the Lamanites. Do you or Seth have any ideas?"

There was again silence as the men considered. Finally Seth responded.

"Sir, why don't we just ignore it? If the Lamanites ask anything, they are more likely to ask if we have captured any of the priests yet—and you can honestly answer that we have not. That seems to be their major concern."

The king nodded. "Very well, then."

Just then Lammonihah entered the room, bringing with him not only his guard detail, but also the four young men and several others. Ammon introduced them to the king, who took notice of their exhaustion.

"Seth, call Omer and have food brought."

When Omer returned with the servants, it was plain he was curious about what was going on. But he was too much the courtier to ask questions. Instead he kept his ears and eyes open, trying to find out as much as he could himself.

The new arrivals finally finished eating, and the king gave orders for them to be housed. "Lammonihah, take them with you."

But before he could continue, Gideon interrupted. "Pardon, sir, but is that really wise?"

With a frown on his face, Limhi indicated that he should continue.

"There is only one place where the men can be as safe as we can make them, sir, and that is here in the palace. Sometimes the Lamanite captain has dropped by the barracks, and it would be difficult to explain away the new faces—especially since there are no other new recruits."

The king nodded. "You make a good point, Gideon." Turning towards Seth, he continued. "Very well, then, Seth, you know where the guest chambers are. Command Omer to prepare them and then take these men there."

As the new arrivals left, Limhi asked Ammon and the other three to come closer.

"Tomorrow I plan to issue a proclamation to my people to gather together. I wish to share with them the news that you have brought." Raising his hand to stop Gideon's comments, he continued. "It will take a few days for the word to get around and the people to gather. I wish to use that time to work out a plan of escape, as I indicated to you earlier."

Ammon nodded. "Perhaps, if you can tell me of the ways you have already considered, we can give you some help."

Time passed quickly as the group began discussing problems and possible means of escape.

Chapter 9

The gathering day finally arrived. As Limhi began to approach the meeting place with his guards, he noticed that Gideon looked worried.

"What is the problem, my friend?"

Gideon looked around anxiously. "I cannot help but think that when the Lamanites hear—and I'm certain they will...."

Limhi nodded. "They already have."

"What?!" Gideon was shocked.

"I sent a messenger to the Lamanite king, telling him that I wanted to gather my people together—to preach to them. I did not tell him what I would be preaching about."

"But...." Gideon found himself at a loss for words.

"I plan on us being gone before he receives a full report—and certainly before he can come against us with an army!"

Gideon just shook his head in silence. The king looked over at him and continued.

"I felt it was safer, and wiser, to give him at least some information. This way, he cannot accuse us of going behind his back. And I have gained us a little bit of time."

There were many, many people gathered together. As the king mounted the platform, conversations stopped, and they turned their attention to Limhi.

"O my people," he began, "lift up your heads and be comforted. The time is not far away when we shall no longer be slaves to our enemies, even though our previous attempts have been in vain."

Cries of hope began to sound throughout the crowd. Gideon again shook his head, concerned about the reaction of the Lamanite soldiers.

"Lift up your heads and rejoice, and put your trust in the God of Abraham and Isaac and Jacob—that God who brought the children of Israel out of Egypt through the Red Sea and who fed them in the wilderness. He is the same God who brought our fathers out of the land of Jerusalem and who has kept his people, even until now.

"It is our own iniquities and sins that have brought us into bondage. At this time, we pay tribute to the king of the Lamanites—even one half of our corn and barley and of our grain of every kind and one half of the increase of our flocks and herds. This is hard for us to bear. And our affliction is great. Behold, we have great reason to mourn!

"Many of our brethren have been slain—and all because of our sins. For if we had not fallen into evil, the Lord would not have allowed this great trouble to come upon us. But we would not listen to the words of God; instead, great arguments arose among us, to the point that we even killed each other!

"And we have killed a prophet of the Lord, a man who told of our wickedness, and who prophesied of many things, even the coming of Christ."

Gideon remembered the words that he had heard Abinadi preach.

"This prophet said that Christ was God, the Father of all things. He would take upon himself the image of man—that God would take upon himself flesh and blood and go forth upon the face of the earth.

"Because of this, and for many other reasons, the Lord has brought his wrath upon us. He has said, 'I will not help my people in the day of their transgressions, but I will make their way difficult so that they do not prosper. If my people will sow filthiness, they shall reap the east wind, which brings immediate destruction.'"

There was silence for a moment while the people thought about what Limhi had said. Then someone called out, "But what can we do?"

Limhi continued. "We have seen that the promise of the Lord is fulfilled; you yourselves are afflicted by the Lamanites. But if you will turn to the Lord with full purpose of heart, and put your trust in him, and serve him with all of your mind, he will deliver you out of this bondage, according to his own will and pleasure."

A roar of approval greeted this statement. Taking advantage of the moment, Limhi turned to call Ammon up beside him.

"This man has come from our brethren who are in the land of Zarahemla. I have asked him to share with you all that has happened."

Ammon looked out over the crowd. He saw far more women and children than there were men, and realized again this was because of the battles Limhi had referred to. Quickly he gathered his thoughts together and then began to share with the people all that had happened from the time that Zeniff, Limhi's grandfather, had left Zarahemla until the time that he and his brothers had left.

As he finished that report, he looked over to the king, who nodded to him to continue.

"I also wish to share with you the final words that our king, Benjamin, taught us. They also teach of Christ, and of the way that we ought to behave towards one another."

The meeting lasted well into the afternoon, as Ammon continued his teachings in simple words that the people could understand. When he had finished, Limhi stood again.

"There is much for us to think on. It is time, now for all of you to return to your homes. Ponder these words; think on all those things we have shared today."

Slowly the crowd began to break up. Parents and children began to gather themselves together and slowly make up groups to return to their homes.

Gideon ordered some of his men to roam the area, making themselves available to help in whatever way needed. As he wandered, he was stopped several times by people wanting to know how they were going to be free.

"There are so many Lamanites and so few of us. We cannot fight for our freedom."

When Limhi and his attendants returned to the palace, he again called Seth, Gideon, Ammon and his brothers, and a few other trusted friends together. Seth spoke first.

"My lord, how can we free ourselves? The people are willing, but there are so many of the Lamanites and so few of us."

Gideon nodded. "That is the statement I heard over and over today, my lord."

Limhi agreed. "But that is not why I want to visit at this moment." He turned to Ammon. "Ammon, how can we enter into a covenant with God to keep his commandments? Can you and your brothers baptize us?"

Ammon shook his head. "I am an unworthy servant, my lord. I do not have the authority to do that, although I can teach."

"Then we must wait," the king went on. "Will you continue to teach us?"

"Surely!" Ammon agreed. "But, my lord, the best thing we can do right now is to determine how to release you and your people from bondage."

Suddenly Limhi yawned. "I agree—but I don't think we will accomplish anything while we are tired. I think it would be better for us to sleep now and meet again in the morning."

The small group disbanded, each full of his own thoughts. When they gathered the next morning, Gideon stood before the king.

"O king, you have listened to my words many times when we have been fighting with the Lamanites. If you have found them to be helpful to you, listen to me now, and I will deliver this people out of bondage."

Limhi looked tired, but at Gideon's words, his face came alive. "Speak, Gideon, speak!"

Gideon continued. "You remember the pass through the back wall, on the far side of the city? The guards of the Lamanites there are often drunk at night. So let us send a proclamation among all the people that they gather together the flocks and herds to drive them into the wilderness by night. And I will go, according to your command, and pay the last wine tribute to the Lamanites. They will get drunk, and we can pass through the secret pass on the left of their camp when they are drunk and asleep."

The king looked around, waiting for any reaction. But no one spoke. "I see no other way, Gideon. I had forgotten the pass—surely the Lord has put it into your mind. Seth, call Omer."

The little man scurried into the presence of the king. Limhi stared hard at him.

"Omer, I want a proclamation sent throughout the entire land, ordering my people to gather together their flocks. They are to keep them together three nights from now, for that is when we will leave."

Omer's face turned pale. "Leave, my lord? How?"

"That is not for you to know, Omer. But this much you must know—if one word of this leaks to the Lamanites, I will know where it comes from."

Omer shook his head. "No, lord, my lips are sealed."

Limhi smiled rather grimly. "They had better be—or they will be sealed permanently! Now go. Tell the people to gather their flocks, their gold, their silver, and all the precious things they can carry. They must gather together provisions for the journey, too."

As Omer scurried from the room, Limhi turned to Gideon. "What else do we need to do?"

Gideon paused in thought for a moment. "I will need the tribute wine—and it would be advisable to send that much more wine, as a present."

Limhi nodded. "It shall be done."

"Then it is just a question of waiting—and praying that the Lamanites do not get suspicious."

Gideon and Seth went out on the streets daily, watching for any suspicions on the part of the Lamanites. But their eyes seemed to be blind to all of the activity that the two Nephites could see going on around them.

On the morning of the third day, Gideon called a detail of soldiers together. As they gathered, he issued his commands.

"We will take the tribute wine to the soldiers at the gates. And we will take this extra wine to the soldiers at the back gate—as a present from the king."

Although he could see the questions in their eyes, Gideon chose not to say anything else. Instead, he picked up his portion of the burden, waited for the rest to do the same, and began the deliveries.

He found he had to bite his tongue as the Lamanites this day seemed to take particular delight in mocking him. "So, Gideon, the great warrior, has been reduced to making deliveries!" "Here comes the great soldier, carrying wineskins! What's the matter, Gideon? Has the king lost his trust in you?"

Gideon knew it would not take much for the soldiers to lose their tempers. So after each delivery, he reminded them of their orders. "There is to be absolutely no response to any of the jibes! None, whatsoever. You are to deliver the wine, and that is all. Are there any questions?"

There were none, and the deliveries continued. At the last one—the soldiers at the back gate—the mocking grew worse. Gideon felt his face turn red as the Lamanite soldiers accused him and his men of cowardice and everything else they could think of. But when he began to unload the extra wine, the comments changed.

"My lord the king has thought that you might be thirsty and has sent this extra wine as a present."

Shouts and cheers arose at this. "He's learning! Maybe we'll let him stay on yet!" The Lamanites grabbed at the wine sacks, and Gideon thankfully motioned his men to return to the barracks.

That evening as it grew dark, Limhi and his friends again gathered together.

"Are all the people ready, Gideon?"

"As ready as they can be, my lord. My men have been helping whenever they can."

"And what of the guards? Has your plan worked?"

"I have had someone on watch all day, sir. The Lamanites have thoroughly enjoyed the present you sent. There will be no trouble."

At that moment Omer entered. His face was pale and his knees were shaking.

"My lord, there is a soldier who says he must see you." Limhi turned impatiently to the chamberlain. "Then bring him in, Omer."

"Yes, sir." The little man backed out of the room, looking fearfully about him.

Limhi spoke softly. "I wonder how many of my people are fearful of leaving...even the safety of slavery."

The soldier entered. "My lord, I was told to report to you when the guards had gone to sleep. The time is now, sir."

Limhi turned to Gideon. "Well, my friend. It looks like now is the time we put our trust *completely* in God."

"Yes sir. Are your people all ready?"

"I hope so." Raising his voice, he called, "Omer!" Again the little man scurried in.

"Yes, my lord."

"Omer, gather together any who are left here. It is time to leave."

"Yes...yes, sir." The little man began to back away.

"And Omer, remind them that this is their only chance."

Limhi, Gideon, Ammon and the others made their way to the back gate. It seemed impossible for the Lamanites not to hear the noise of the crowd, but no soldiers appeared on the street.

At the gate, Gideon took charge. He sent soldiers to help divide the people into more manageable groups. When this was done, he gave the order to open the secret pass, and the people began to pour out the gate. Some began to cheer, but Gideon quickly sent runners to order it stopped.

"God is helping us—but we must do our part as well! We must go as silently as we can."

Finally everyone was through. Gideon breathed a sigh of relief as he turned and saw the last group come out of the city.

Turning to Limhi, he said, "My lord, my part of our journey has ended. Now where do we go?"

Limhi turned to Ammon. "You must direct us now, Ammon. We trust in you to bring us to the land of Zarahemla—and to a place of peace."

Ammon paused and looked around. Sheep were bleating and cattle lowing. Children were crying, and there were the constant noises that belong to a large group of people.

"Sir, before we go further, I would like to ask God's blessing on our trip."

Limhi nodded. The word was passed through the throng, and gradually they became as quiet as could be expected.

"O God," Ammon began. "We pause now to ask your blessing on our journey. You have brought us safely to this point; we trust you to bring us safely to the end. We praise you for your goodness in bringing us back together, and in letting us share your good news with these our new friends. Now we go forth in faith, in the name of your Son who is to come, even Jesus Christ. Amen."

When he ended, King Limhi, Gideon, and Ammon set out at the head of the people, journeying to a new land of promise and freedom. Behind them they left broken dreams and soldiers who would never understand what had happened to their prisoners.